SPORTS PAGES

Poetry by Arnold Adoff

Birds
Black is brown is tan
friend dog
i am the running girl
Where Wild Willie
The Poetry of Black America:
Anthology of the 20th Century

SPORTS PAGES

by Arnold Adoff

illustrations by Steve Kuzma

J. B. Lippincott   New York

Library of Congress Cataloging-in-Publication Data
Adoff, Arnold.
    Sports pages.

    Summary: Poems about the experiences and feelings
of young athletes involved in various sports.
    1. Sports—Juvenile poetry. 2. Children's poetry,
American. [1. Sports—Poetry. 2. American poetry]
I. Kuzma, Steve, ill.   II. Title.
PS3551.D66S6 1986   811'.54   85-45169
ISBN 0-397-32102-3
ISBN 0-397-32103-1 (lib. bdg.)

Always for Jaime, Leigh and Title IX

I   Move   From   Sport   To   Sport.

Alone   in my head   during the final heat of the big race,
            or anchored in my place   as our team moves through
those final moments   between a victory   and a sad defeat:
        I move from sport to sport   as the seasons change,
                                            as we change
                                    and   bend   and   grow.

I   learn.
We learn.   I   know a dream can become reality.
            We know a dream can remain a dream.

Alone   in my head   or taking my place   as part of a team,
        I sweat and worry.   I smile away the nagging fear.
There is always hard work, but near the end of each final
        practice session, I know I am ready to do my final
                                                        best.
                        Win   or   lose   I will do well.

I am getting stronger   the longer I play.

I am getting better each day. I can tell.

Alone In The Nets.

I

am

alone   of   course,

in the nets, on this cold and raining afternoon,

and our best defending fullback

is lying on the wet ground   out of position.

Half the opposition is pounding

down the field,

and their lead forward is gliding

so fast, she can just barely keep

the ball in front of her   sliding

foot.

Her cleats are expensive,

and her hair $b_ou_nc_es$

neatly

like the   after
girls   in the shampoo commercials.

There   is   a   big   grin

on her face.

Now: In This Frozen Moment On This Moving World Through Space

is the right time to ask why am I here   just standing

in my frozen place?

Why   did I get up on time this morning?

Why   did I get up at all?

Why   did I listen to the coach and agree to play

this strange position in a r e a l game

in a strange town   on this wet and moving world?

Why is it raining?

Why is it raining so h a r d?

Where

are all of our defenders?

Why do all of our players

do all of the falling

down?

Why am I here?

But Frozen Moments Can Unfreeze And I Can Stretch

and reach for the ball   flying to the corner of

                                          our

                                          goal.

I can reach   and jump
               and d i v e   into the s p a c e

                            between my out
                                  stretched
                                    hands

and the outside poles

        of the nets.

My fears evaporate   like my sweat in this chilling

                                          breeze,

and I can move with this moving world

and pace my steps

like that   old
              movie

        high
        noon   sheriff   in his just

                          right

                          time.

That grinning forward gets her shot away too soon,
and I am there, on my own time, in the air,
                    to meet the ball,
and fall on it
for   the save.

I wave my happy ending wave and get up.
                    The game   goes on.

Watch Me On The Wing.

Sweeper: the deeper I can play
　　　　the faster I can lay
out my traps for their fullback
moving too close to mid   field.
I shine along the side   lines
　　　　　from mid field
　　　　back to our goal.

I am the quickest,
　　　sharpest,
most   intelligent,
(and
most m o d e s t ,) player on
　　　　　　　　　my
　　　　　　　team:
　　　　in this league.

14

I have the

superspeed:

I have the need to do a little

more

than play only one position. I

defend. I score. I run like

wind

across the corn fields   of

this

town.

I am a brown tornado on a

muddy

day.

The opposition knows

I come to play   with

all I bring. They

watch:

w a t c h   m e   o n   t h e   w i n g .

15

Prohibited Acts: Attacking From The Rear. Kicking.   Tripping.

Hitting   or

punching.

Holding.   Pushing.

Roughness.

Using the hands or

arms

intentionally.

Dangerous or wild

play.

Interference.

Blocking with the

shoulder. Kicking

the   ball from the

goalie's hands.

Illegally

attacking

the goalie.

Attacking

the

goalie.

Though The Afternoon Was Freezing Cold,

there was a place
in front   of   the
                  nets
that was soft and
           dug out.

When the cleats
on my right foot
caught   in that
           soft
                  mud,
my body was
already   turning
   and following
   into the play.
My right knee
                  was
                  turning
                  too.

Only my foot
remained
        unmoving
in its   unmoving
            shoe.

This was   definitely   not   a   good   day.

My Knee Is Only Sprained,

            is   only   swollen,
and
the doctor says   I will be
                              fine.
              I'll play again.

            He says this as he
            sits   on his padded
            leather chair that
            can swivel   360 de
                              grees.
            Oh
                why can't knees?

Still.   We do not make the Six O'Clock News
         with this old story, often told, of
              pain and frustration and fear.
Still.
         I must sit on this bench   and be as
still as this brace demands;
         as
still as the other spectators   behind me   in
                              the stands.
I have been told: next season,
                next y e ar.

20

21

Wrestling The Beast.

This guy is an animal. A pig?   Squealing sinus breathing.

                       A bear?   Hair on his fat arms.

                       A dog?   No, not biting, but his

                                                 c h i n

                                  digging into my collar

                                                    bone.

A dragon. Easy. Dragon breath.

An anaconda snake. His mistake:

choke hold around my neck.

                       A jackal? A hyena? A hungry lion?

                       A wounded   tiger

                                  alone in the dark bush?

A bee?

An

   ant? A worm? A toad? A dying fly on the end of a frog's

                                                      tongue?

This guy is an animal. A gentle cat rolled

                               - over

                       by me.

                       O n e.

                       T w o.

                       Three.

23

Coach Says: Listen Sonny, You Are The Safety On This Team,
And Your Body Belongs To Me, And Your Safety Is The Last
Thing On Your Mind. Right? Right. Their Guy Is Super Fast.
Do Not Let Him Get Past. Period. Understood? Safety   Last.
Now Play It By The Numbers.

Simple.

    We start with eleven when the whistle blows,

and

      their quarterback throws his pass.

                 Simple.

Number One: He throws the ball.

Number Two: The ball is caught.

Number Three: Their receiver runs

                d o w n   the field

                      toward me.

Number Four

Through Ten: My team

             mates who ought to stop him   are hit

       or

        fall, or miss, or are too slow to make

                         the play.

Simple.

    Safety last. I am the last of our eleven,

        and the runner runs my way.

Afternoons: One.

The way I am playing this position, I must look like a full back with half a brain. I am too slow. I need a heatrub fix. I am far beyond some green water and a heavily advertised candy bar. Even though I tend to exaggerate during emotional situations, this is the crucial last long moment of this crucial game.

Just when I need that just right word, or clear fact of strategy that might help me get past their monster tackle and lug the ball into the endzone of victory and personal glory, I look toward my bench and blink: I see coach turn his back on me.

Oh

please forgive this bitter moment of mine as my face disappears into the mud of the one yard line.

Afternoons: Two.

No one owns
a foot ball
on   this
          street.
We roll the
morning
          paper
and
tie it with
          old
               rope
and
hope it
          holds
through   the
tough
passing
game.

When you catch my pass   you tuck this paper
in your gut   and make your feet deliver the
                              winning news.

Afternoons: Three.

On the FourthOfJuly
up
on   the   town
           hill   there
                   are
swimming
        and
diving
           races   and
                     a
bike rodeo around
                   the
                   park.

We have to
run
red markers through
a safety course and
clock our times. We
play catch and sack
                race
and   learn
                a
        batch of games
where
        no   one   loses
        no   one   wins.
We
pop our wheelies un
                til
        dark.

Point Guard.

You bring the ball down the court.
The pick is set.
The play is set. The movement of
the ball
is faster
than all
the
d e f e n s i v e
hands and heads,
and you
get free.
You pass into the big girl
at the key. She turns
and
shoots and scores.

The crowd roars.

Sweet.

You are at the line. You take a deep breath.
                          You take a deep breath.

You know: a   free   throw
                          is really
          a   free   throw:
                          no hands in your face;
                          no race   down
                                      the court;
                          no block,
                          no clock.

This is the place   to score. This is the time to pour   it in,
          and beat those   nasty bad guys   on the   other   team,
                                          once   and   for   all.
This is the time to win   this   game.

You bounce the ball once, and wish   for all the luck
                          you know   you   don't need.
You shoot,   and the ball
          flies
                    and   arcs   and speeds   down   through
                          the hoop   to meet the net.

You get   your point; your score; your wish.   Swish.

Sweet.

My
Short
Story.

I just can't shoot over the shoulders and arms and hands
of this monster-with-a-smile who is their center tonight.
He swats my shots like so many slow motion flies floating
near his head. My dunk is dead. He is too tall. Period.

  He

is a wall of meat in short pants. I just know he must

                                            shave

                        after every meal:

                        six times a day.

How can the refs let him play

against my short-legged self?

I feel like some Santa's elf.

My

sweet jump

            shot hits him in the numbers

                    on his   chest.

                    How do you drive around

                    an 18-wheeling semi for

                    a lay up shot? You

                                        do

                                        not

                                        !

I just can't pass this test

                this

                game.

I just can't shoot.

I just can't score.

My

short

story is a bore.

Afternoons: Four.

Milkshake with eggs:
my legs up on the
                    table
as the screen shows
slow motion secrets
of my favorite pros.
I dream with o p e n
                    e y e s
my future d r e a m:
the new K a r e e m.

Even The Light Seems Dark

      as it comes in through the dirty windows of the gym.
The afternoon is darkening into evening, and I am
                  still at work at these machines:
lifting and pulling
t h e s e   weights   until   my shirt is dark   with   sweat.

Then: I get up from the mats   and run

        up and down the school stairs: f i r s t floor to third,

                      third 'floor to f i r s t,

    over and over   and over again.

Then: I do road running and stretching and road   running,

    again

    until   true

        dark   and the pale moon begins   to   r i s e .

Then. Look: no surprise. I am getting stronger,

                am stronger.

                Strong.

   You want to see muscle:

      here is muscle.

   You want to see leg:

      here is leg.

Now I think it's time to bend this toughened knee,

and b e g   the coach to let me play   on Saturday.

My Team Without Me.

Rough turf,

or an icy surface

              patch

on some strange

              field,

and I can twist

my ankle just
             like
            that.

Or a cheap hit

(from my blind

           side,)

can knock

me flat and

          r i p

my

        last good knee.

And I will sit on benches

through the longest games

in darkening afternoons,

that I have ever had to

    stay seated through,

and

      only

    see.

43

Exercises: To Be Done Each Day.

1. 30 jumping jacks.
2. 10 windmills.
3. 5 leg crossovers: each leg.
4. 25 leg switches: mountain climbing.
5. 10 hamstring pulls.
6. Trunk rotations.
7. 8 push-ups.
8. 30 sit-ups.
9. Hurdle-stretches.
10. 20 toe-risers.
11. Arm circles.
12. Neck rotations.

Week Before A Monday Meet:

Sunday And Wednesday.   Exercises.

Jog 4 minutes. Run 6 minutes at 1/2 speed.
Walk 2 minutes. Repeat 2 times.

Run 3 minutes at 3/4 speed.
Walk 2 minutes. Repeat 3 times.

Run 60 seconds: hard.
Walk 60 seconds. Repeat 2 times.

Run 5–10 minutes.

Sprint at end.

Jog 6 minutes to cool down.

Monday And Thursday.   Exercises.

Jog 4 minutes: easy.

Run 10 minutes: nonstop. Walk 3 minutes.

Run 60 seconds at 3/4 speed.

Walk 60 seconds.

Repeat 4 times.

Run 5 minutes as hard as you can.

Jog 6 minutes to cool down.

Tuesday And Friday.   Exercises. Jog 5 minutes: easy.

Run 4 minutes at 3/4 speed.

Jog 4 minutes: nonstop. Repeat 3 times.

Run 45 seconds. Walk 60 seconds.

Repeat 4 times.

Run 8 minutes: nonstop. Sprint at end.

Jog 6 minutes to cool down.

Saturday. Warm up. Exercises. Run 20 minutes: nonstop.

Sunday. R e l a x. E a t i c e c r e a m.

YOU

        begin to run
             when
SHE   is almost up
               to
YOU.

YOU   are both moving.
YOU   are staying in
            your
            l a n e .
YOU   are picking up
            speed.

SHE   is stretching
            to
reach your
        retreating
          back,
          and

YOU need
to stretch your
left arm back,
and feel her
smack that baton
into the palm
of your hand,
and
YOU are
off as
fast
as
YOU can sprint.

Afternoons: Five.

On saturday afternoons the downtown community center
gets free   passes to SkateWorld. We spend the d a y
playing   crack the whip   and tag   and bragging   back
                                                       ward
to the heavy metal beat. Our feet flash
                    in mirrored
                          lights.

51

Mixed Singles.

She tosses the tennis ball   high

                           into   the   air.
Her
racket comes down harder than I   e v e r

                                      k n e w
a
racket could hit.

It
is a serve into the inside corner,
that I barely see: kicking   chalk
as
it flies away, untouched by   me

I know this will be love.

Ground

Bound

I

watch:

I hold

my

breath

for

my

bend

ing

friend

on

the

par

all

els.

Even
when I
spot
here
from
this
side I
take
this
balance
r
 i
  d
   e
    .

Dear Horse:

        you want this apple.
        and I
            want that
                competition cup.
You
know how to hold your head
            up   straight.
I
know how to post so right,
I could hold   a glass
of water   in my hand
and not spill a drop.

Please   watch out for pheasants
flying up under your nose. Don't
get thirsty just yet.   Keep
                rabbits off
                y o u r   toes.

D o n ' t
    s t o p.

Last Frame

of
this game called
          slow
          pitch:
and
I
whip that
          ball sofast,
               even
                    under
                    hand,

her bat

is much

too

late

to meet   my

throw

across the   plate.

Third strike.

Third o u t .

I

love that l a s t

great

shout.

Last   frame.

End of   game.

There Is A Very Ugly

bruise
on the right
     side   of   my
     right
     knee;
and
an o ther very ug
            ug
            ugly
bruise
on the right
     side   of   my
     right
     arm;
but the
     charm bracelet on my wrist shines new
     and sweet as I sip my soda and smile
     into a certain pair of BigBrown eyes
            this friday afternoon.

What a great time to be a girl.

These Knees:

these   joints: these soft and floating combinations
            of cartilage and ligament and bone:
these   knees
              were
            made   to bend and flex and
                                   run
            the power of thigh and
                     le g
                        muscles
                        together,
            at the instant
            of the   starting
                     gun.

These knees were never made to be hit by shoulder pads,
            or helmets, or the f l y
                           i n g   bodies   of
                              young   heroes,
                              and   heroines:
         impressing   home
                     town
                     fans.

Equal Curses On Two Long Lines Of Equally Short Ancestors.

Because I am so short, I will crouch down at the plate

and

bend my knees, and try to fool the umpire,

to fool the pitcher

into pitching pitches

outside,

so I can get on base.

Equal curses on that giant of a pitcher,

and his own long lines of ancestors.

Because I am so short, I hate to swing that bat and miss.

I hate to strike out and   listen

to my team

mates groan and

shout.

I want to run and hide.

64

If the ball comes close inside, I won't   jump
away.
I stay within
my crouch,
even
if it hits my
knee.

Equal curses on ancestors and pitchers
and pitches   and
on
me.

One Finger Along The Seam Of The Ball,

or

one finger   across the seam of the ball. Either way

you

will be throwing fast balls.

Strikes:

time after time.

Remember: it is in the speed,

or

in taking a

little

off

the speed.

Throw straight. Don't aim. Try and throw the   same

way

time after time.

Think of the flapping of wings   through the air,

or things with fins

moving through   water

the way the   ball moves through   air.

We always need the wins but your   elbow

is much too

young

for   the   curve.

Catcher.

I am always heavy. This mask is pulling down my head. This chest protector feels like some kind of concrete ball deflector.

These shin guards slow my running
Toward first with the faked throw.　　　I am always late to

　　　　　　　　　　　　　　　　　the back stop,

　　　　　　　　　　　　　　to chase foul balls

　　　　　　　　　　　　　　　　for easy outs.

All my movements　are short and heavy　behind the plate.
I am the battery mate　for the pitcher. I signal the

　　　　　　　　　　　pitcher. I signal the

　　　　　　　　　　　pitch;　　signal

　　　　　　　　　　　　　　w h i c h

infielder will move behind

　　　　　　　　　second

　　　　for the pick o f f
　　　　　　　　　play.

I am always heavy
in my heavy crouch. But when that slick runner comes on
in from third, and I have the ball　in my mitt, waiting
for his heavy hit,
I am the catcher: rooted to the ground for all it takes.
I hold on to the ball and make the out.

Being　heavy　is what it's all　about.

My Left Foot Is Always Near The Bag.

First base. I am ready with my glove
to field grounders, or

hard

hit

line drives.
I am ready
to take the throw and

step

on

first

base
to   get   the   runner   o u t.

I am ready to put the

tag

on
an ankle or foot or toe,
and hold on to the ball
and not let go   until

the

umpire's

shout.

My left foot is always   near the bag.

I Am The   Best Second
             Base Person

                            on this team, but I play short
                                                    stop,
                            because my arm   is better than
                            any
                            of our   other player's   best.
                            You know
                                        the
                                        other
                            teams have put it to the test.

I can burn my throws straight to first,
and light up the hand
                            inside that first
                                        base
                                        man's
                                        glove.
I love it   when the guy yells:
                            OW!
        G O O D   T H R O W!

I know
    that
    loud
respect.

72

Sometimes In Center Field On A Hot Summer Evening,

when the air is so still   you almost think you hear
                  the mosquitos warming up their engines,
and
our pitcher is getting
the o p p o s i t i o n
to dribble grounders
        to the infield.

        . .

Sometimes   in center field
I have a hard time staying
                awake.
I never
    close my eyes and fall asleep standing,
            but my mind will m o v e
                        o v e r
to last week's extra-inning loss
and my wild toss to third to
                help
them score and help *us* lose that g a m e.

My throat is always too dry
and there is always an ice
cold
can
of pop waiting at the cold
pop
stand.

One time a well-hit ball popped into my outstretched hand
before I could remember my name.

Two

Out   In The Bottom Of The Ninth,

and   this   is   the   s l o w m o t i o n   part   of   the   movie.

I

am   in   the   movie,   near   the   end   of   a   long   game.

the   announcer   is   calling   my   name.   The   fans   are   calling

                                    my   name.   The   ball   is   flying

                                    s l o w l y   over   my   head   as

I   run   s   l   o   w   l   y

          u   n   d   e   r   it: catch   up   with   it   at   the   far   fence.

In   this   moment   of   s l o w   suspense   no   one   knows   how   it

                                                will   all   come   out.

The   announcer   and   the   fans   and

                              the

          coach   all   wait.

     The   hitter   waits.

               I   wait   too.

But

my   feet   have   left   the   ground   and   my   arm   is   stretching

                              higher   than   the   flying   ball.

Then it is all over, and the movie moves ahead: the

ball

is in my glove, and I am s i t t i n g on

the out

field

green.

The game is over, and I imagine   my name

heads the credits spread across s o m e

imaginary

screen.

78

We   Have   Our   Moments.

Sometimes   we leap and land.
Sometimes   we trip and fall.
Sometimes   we catch the other team   before they score.
Sometimes   we jump too soon   and get faked out of our
socks.

We can be sharp on the pick-off play at third.
    Or
        we can have rocks in our heads and miss that
            softly batted ball,
            and miss that
            one
            sweet chance to
            save
            the
            day.

I lose. I win. We lose. We win.
The team   finishes   in last place.
The team is
        in the play-offs at last
        and past defeats f a d e
            fast.

We   have   our   moments.

79